KICKING the ODDS

My Dream, Vision and Reality of Becoming a Rockette

———

MarQue Munday

Kicking the Odds

This book contains memories as a Radio City Rockette. The information is anecdotal and derives from my time as a Rockette. It contains information I learned as a Rockette tour guide. This book also includes stories about experiences that were either witnessed by me or shared by my Rockette sisters.

ISBN 978-0-9905593-6-8

Printed in USA

Published in the United States by Thee MarQuee Publishing subsidiary of Thee MarQuee Enterprises, Inc.

Cover Design: MarQue Munday & Kevin Vain – KDV & Associates
Editor: Jennifer Dowdle – Rockette Alumnae

Foreword by: Walter E Jones – Former Mighty Morphin Power Ranger (Zack – Black Ranger)

Dedication

This book is dedicated to all of the dreamers in the world. Dreaming is one of life's best outlets. The world has enough reality going on; it's time to take a few moments to dream. When we use our dreams wisely, we have the ability to change a piece of the world's reality, namely our own. So, why wait? Dream big. Visualize. Set goals. Write them down. Keep a journal. Spend five to ten minutes each day allowing yourself to dream. Imagine whatever you want. Nothing is too outlandish; as a matter of fact, the crazier the visions, the better. You will be surprised how your dreams can transform your reality. Let the dreamers of the world unite.

Table of Contents

Foreword

I met MarQue Munday in college at the United States International University School of Performing and Visual Arts. I was a kid from Detroit, MI, far from home. I had made the decision to come to California to alleviate the burden on my single mom. It was time to grow up and become a man. MarQue was this beautiful dancer, singer, and actress from New York when we met. She was bigger than life to me, with long legs, a lovely smile, and a hunger to grow and learn. She came from a different lifestyle than mine. She spoke highly of her family and their support for her pursuits. She captivated me with her zest for learning and her determination to make a mark. She was organized; she set goals. MarQue took her life seriously. As time passed our friendship grew. We performed together in shows and encouraged each other to reach our fullest potential. Opportunities to acquire stand-out roles in musicals were uncommon at our school. Despite the odds, we had dreams of dazzling on the stage.

MarQue eventually embarked on other paths, and we were out of touch for a while. While visiting New York City for an appearance on a hit show called, The Mighty Morphin Power Rangers, we reconnected. She invited me to watch her Radio City performance as a Rockette. I proudly attended The Radio City Christmas Spectacular and beamed as I watched my friend. MarQue was the only "carmel girl" on that Great Stage, yet she blended consonantly with the other women's flawless long-legged precision. Watching MarQue on that stage awakened a realization. She and I had both broken barriers in this business of show people. As she glided elegantly across that legendary stage, her smile reached the back of the theatre, fueled by a pride that only a barrier-breaker could summons.

MarQue's continued growth has not surprised me. Recently, I bumped into her in Australia, while attending a theatrical production featuring, *Songs in the Key of Motown*. To my delight, MarQue, radiant in her glory, was singing and performing on that stage. After the show, I shocked her with my presence. We were both thrilled at this serendipitous reunion. Oh, how good life is! Since that chance meeting, MarQue and I have remained in contact with each other. Her latest project, this book, will inspire others to chase their dreams. MarQue, I continue to be inspired by your talents and tenacity. This book will guide others to achieve the great moments life offers. To all who read this book, remember, "Life is the adventure you create for yourself." Let the reading and your adventures commence!

-   Walter Emanuel Jones

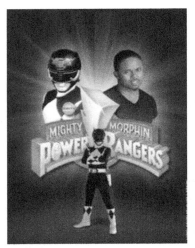

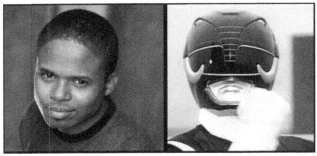

Preface

This book is a reflection of my dreams. As a young child, I was told that if I was willing to work hard enough, I could achieve anything. Being a child, I took that literally and put my mind right to work. Later, at the age of 12, I was introduced to the "Silva Mind" technique at a Jose Silva - Silva Mind Seminar. During this seminar, we were given instruction on memorization and visualization skills. Once again, I took this information and applied it literally, expecting nothing less than results. As I applied the Silva tools and techniques consistently, they became second nature. The challenge occurred when I started interacting with other children my age. Negative peer influences were powerful, and the impact of peers, who lacked the Silva perspective, thwarted my dreams for a period of time. The wonderful truth is that one can apply these Silva principles anytime to hone mental focusing skills. Having learned to trust my inner voice, I continue to dream and develop a "laundry list" of aspirations that will come to fruition in the near future. This book is not only a testament to my dream fulfillment, but it also serves as a reflection on my life's journey. The purpose of this book is to inspire, encourage and move you to dream.

If you believe, you will achieve and receive an extraordinary life of passion and purpose; your dream life!
#DLYDL

Chapter One

The Beginning of a DREAM

Like many little girls, I started dancing at age 3. I studied ballet and tap at Mrs. Rosemary's Dance Studio on Arthur Avenue in Staten Island, NY, my hometown. I grew up in what they call "the suburbs" of New York City. What I find funny is that many people in New York City have never been to Staten Island and vice versa. However, Mrs. Rosemary was unique and set much higher standards for all of her dancers. She provided us with opportunities to study and audition in The Big Apple. Many of Mrs. Rosemary's teachers had auditioned for the famous Radio City Music Hall Rockettes. As everyone knows, becoming a Rockette, was the pinnacle of every dancer's dreams. Radio City Music Hall, 1560 6th Avenue, NYC has been the home to The Rockettes since 1932. The Rockettes are an American Institution, comparable to baseball, apple pie and the Chevrolet.

In 1925, Russell Markert founded the Rockettes, originally called *The Missouri Rockets*. Over the next seven years, Markert embarked on a cross-country tour with these dancing ladies and changed the troupes name to *The Rockets*. While in New York City performing at the Rivoli Theatre, the group was spotted by impresario S.L. Roxy Rothafel who hired them for his Roxy Theatre. From this experience, the dance group became known as *Markert's Roxyettes*. In 1932, Rothafel moved to Radio City Music Hall. His dance group accompanied him, and their name changed for the final time; *The Rockettes* were born.

Markert referred to *The Rockettes* as his "dancing daughters." During performances at the Music Hall, he was known to encourage these performers verbally. He could be found in the wings shouting, "shake it up for Daddy!" Markert remained the Rockettes' director and choreographer until 1971. Upon his retirement, he was presented by his "daughters" with a plaque displaying his bronzed tap shoes that read "Shake it Up for Daddy, Your Dancing Daughters." Since that time, the Rockettes have entertained audiences with their precision, eye-high kicks for over 90 years. Today, more than 100 dancers are considered Rockettes, allowing prolific lines of Rockettes to perform at any given time. The dance troupe's role has expanded to include venues outside of Radio City Music Hall and New York City. The Rockettes' busy schedule has included sporting events, conventions, national tours, film and television appearances. They have also performed with such luminaries as Ann Margaret, Liberace, Chita Rivera, Peter Allen, Susan Anton, Tommy Tune, Rip Taylor, Paige O'Hara, and Maurice Hines. Today that the list of celebrity joint-appearances continues to grow...

From the tender young age of 3, my soul was struck with a desire. I had to become a Rockette. My dance teacher's drive ignited this passion and curiosity. I didn't realize there were no black (Afro-American) Rockettes in the Radio City dancing line, so I saw no limitations to this goal. I went about my young ways – practicing my dance steps incessantly. One day, I would try out, as my dance teachers had done, at Radio City Music Hall. No one could dissuade my ambition, and I danced my heart out daily for the next fifteen years.

Today, as I remember these times, I recall my dad regretting the installation of the tile floor in our bathrooms. I practiced tap steps for hours on end, and the echoing tap sounds annoyed him profusely. But, my dad never asked me to stop tapping. He knew that dance was the key to **discipline** in my life. I loved to dance, and I never missed class. Dance instilled discipline in my life before I was old enough to take on the traditional household chore regiment. Discipline came in the form of my earliest dance practice sessions. At 3 years old, I was still taking naps and only attending half-day kindergarten, yet I already knew to practice my dance steps and to arrive punctually and prepared for class. As time passed and I adopted chores, there were expectations that chores were to be completed before I commencing with play or extracurricular activities (dance). Dance was teaching me more than rhythms and elaborate steps; dance was instructing me about **responsibility**, **consequences** and how to make **choices/decisions.**

Each year, the culmination of our yearly dance training was celebrated with a summer recital. Our families were invited to view the fruits of our labor. We wore fancy sequined dance costumes and brightly tinted make-up. I even made a special trip to the hairdresser, a rare treat, largely because I had an abundance of hair that required hours of taming. These dance recitals were held at the Paramount Movie Theatre, and we performed on a real theatrical stage. As I matured, these recital experiences tumbled me back in time – to a memory that has remained with me. My very first live concert was at Radio City Music Hall. I was a mere 6 years old. My babysitter, Stephanie, accompanied me to a live performance of *The Jackson Five*. I was spellbound by the show, especially the vibrancy of a young Michael Jackson. I remember taking photos relentlessly and an usher asked me, "Haven't you taken enough pictures?" Radio City Music Hall dwarfed the Paramount Theater, but a connection between my dance recitals and Radio City Music Hall was solidified; someday, I would dance on that Great Stage.

By the time I turned 8, my dance skills had advanced rapidly and I had also developed an interest in acting. One night, while watching a favorite family television program called, *Goodtimes,* the character, Penny, played by Janet Jackson, spoke directly to my heart. During her segment, I asked my mother, "Mom do these people live on TV?" My mother explained that the characters were actors who pretend to live together as an inner-city family. I was sold! I wanted to be just like Penny. Eventually, I watched The *Tom Jones Show* where Penny (Janet Jackson) portrayed Mae West with her brother Randy. Penny sang with her brother Randy, and she danced! She even acted as a "little black girl" on television. My mother took notice of my interest in show business and imparted that I could be anything I wanted to become. With five year of dance training under my belt, I believed I was well on my way.

As time passed, I found myself in high school at Staten Island Academy. I was one of three black students in my entire grade. The other two students of color included, Steven, a boy I knew from elementary and junior high school, and Serrae, a new friend I made from Dongan Hills. Serrae and I played basketball, field hockey, softball and tennis together. I continued to dance, while finding time to try cheerleading. Balancing my academics and sports proved challenging, but my dancing was the equalizer. Dance was still my passion. As long as I had dance as my outlet of self-expression, I could balance all aspects of my life. Dance provided

18

peace. When I danced, I freed my mind. Dance was the most natural activity I experienced, aside from breathing. My passion was identified. DANCE was my strong and barely controllable emotion.

By the time I was a junior in high school. I began taking the bus to dance class with my friends. Class was on the other side of the island, and this travel experience presented a new reality to my life: **prejudice** - when people dislike someone simply because he/she is different. As a dedicated dancer, I made sure to head directly to my classes and return home immediately after the class ended. Dilly dallying was not in my routine. I knew being caught after dark on the other side of the island could pose danger. One time, when the bus wasn't scheduled to arrive for at least twenty minutes, my friends and I walked over to a city diner. While enjoying our food, we noticed our bus approaching only a block away. Of all days, our bus arrived early! We bolted out of the diner, dance bags in hand, and raced toward the bus as it pulled away. Screaming for the bus to slow down, we noticed a carload of high school boys hearing us. From the car, we heard the boys chanting, "Niggas!" I will never forget the shame and terror those words evoked in me. The bus driver, having heard the boys' obscenities, stopped in the middle of the block to let us on. I was rattled. Could those stories my parents shared about Skin color be true? For this experience, I extrapolated the reality that my dream of becoming a Rockette was useless. Why had Bernadette, Mrs. Rosemary's exceptionally talented and long-legged dancer been turned down by the Rockettes? Of all the dancers I had known, Bernadette embodied the qualities of the quintessential Rockette. Perhaps her rejection by the "Dancing Daughters" reflected an institutional prejudice? Had Bernadette been white, she most likely would have realized her dream on The Great Stage. And what did this fact mean for me?

Although my legs weren't as long and I wasn't as talented as Bernadette, I still continued dancing. In addition to my dance training, I branched out to study piano and to sing with our church choir. The arts enticed me, and my mother planned a family outing to the stage play, *Don't Bother Me, I Can't Cope.* Other family members nourished my love for the theater with trips to see other shows. My Godmother, aunt Louella, exposed me to the musical, *Your Arms Too Short To Box*

With God. Nothing topped, however, my mother accompanying me to the musical *Dreamgirls.* To this day, *Dreamgirls* remains on of my all-time favorite musicals. What I remember distinctly about all of these shows is the presence of people of color: people who looked just like me. My family gave me exposure to these incredible theatrical events so I could understand the possibility of realizing my dreams as a performer. Without a doubt, I knew there was a place for me in this profession called *"SHOWBIZ".*

The summer of my June graduation from high school, my life took a unique turn. I enlisted in the United States Army and shipped out to Fort Dix, New Jersey. This twist of events was not my idea. My best friend and I had decided to enlist as part of a "buddy system." I needed more discipline if I hoped to ultimately achieve a career in the performing arts. My best friend's father was a career military man who encouraged recent graduate to experience military service. Although my military stint was short-lived, it provided valuable lessons about life, friends and my future. Right away, our "buddy system" failed. The morning my friend and I were scheduled to leave together, the recruiter arrived at my home, bright and early, informing me that my friend would not join us. The night before our scheduled departure, my friend's mom had thrown a thoughtful "going away" party for her. I remember thinking the party was terrific. What had gone wrong in the meantime? The recruiter was not at liberty to discuss my friend's status, and it was too late for me to drop out. I had no choice but to enter the military on my own. About a week and a half later, my friend finally arrived. Unfortunately, we were assigned to different platoons with different service dates. She wouldn't even be in my boot camp graduating class. Through these tenuous circumstances, I learned **perseverance.** With great humility, my time in the military taught me to push ahead and never quit. Tenacity was the only option. My time in the army challenged me and made me reconsider "self-imposed" limitation. In boot camp, I became acquainted with gospel music at Sunday church service. For the first time in my life, I participated in a non-denominational Christian church setting, something completely foreign to my background, having been raised in the Episcopal Church. Boot camp also provided me with my first multi-cultural community. I struggled to adjust to the newness, and my mother sent me the serenity prayer to support my assimilation. I remember the prayer words, "God grant me the strength to accept the things I cannot change, to change the things I can and the wisdom to know the difference." Culture shock and home sickness were my new reality, and I faced this condition without my best friend. I began learning about **trust, honesty, integrity and control**. It was a crash course in life lessons, and I was far from thrilled. I even ended up hospitalized for six days during my boot camp training. Looking back today, despite the hardship I endured during this tumultuous time, I am still reaping the benefits of my service in the military. Discipline, Responsibility, Perseverance, Truth, Honesty, Integrity, (Self) Control, Passion, and **Prayer**. During this most difficult experience, my dreams were transitioning into **visions**. I became more resolved to pursue a showbiz career as a dancer, singer, and actress, after all. And I was ready to get on my way!

With a successful completion of military boot camp, I embraced a new life adventure - college. Just what was I going to study? My parents eagerly awaited my decision. Dance, of course! How could I do anything else? Dance had consumed the majority of my life, with the exception of my infancy. It was my passion and my true love. Remembering the musicals I had digested with family members, I realized a singing, dancing, and acting career was my goal. Challenges immediately surfaced; how do I find a way to pursue these interests, given my commitment to the army? If I registered at the community college, I figured there would be time to sort our the logistics of my long-term plans. My return from boot camp came with fatigue and a sense of discord. Any decision I made about schooling had to be factored into my new monthly obligation to the Army Reserves. I had chosen a path, which allowed me to live a post boot camp life as a civilian for the majority of each month. On one weekend each month, however, I was required to report to my local base to serve the Army Reserves. The following summer, I would be sent to MOS school for training, with a six-year commitment. Upon completion of this work, I would receive money for college. Six years of my life had been signed away, yet I was prepared to continue my education at the community college on Staten Island. To bide time, I enrolled in classes that would interest me, outside of the arts. Courses, such as accounting and business, I quickly realized were not the best fit. Without hesitation, I initiated the transfer process to a school with performing arts classes. My **ambition** was making me restless; I was in limbo and taking too much transition time. To stay focused on my ultimate goals, I tried out for the men's basketball cheerleading squad, in hopes of remaining active, limber and creative. Cheerleading provided a means-to-an-end. It wasn't a replacement for dance, but it provided fun, creative, physical relief. Around this time, my health became a concern and my doctor diagnosed me with rheumatoid arthritis. When the army recruiter came to conduct a physical examination, I presented my doctor's findings. After scrutiny by a military doctor, I received an honorable medical discharge from the army. After one year of military service, I was out. Before I had realized it, my cheerleading season ended, and I was entering Aldelphi University's Dance Department on Long Island. My **drive** and ambition were **relentless**, and I was **determined** to reach my **dreams**.

As a dance major at Adelphi University, I studied dance eight hours each day, five days a week. Classes consisted primarily of ballet and modern. I had never danced so much in my life, but every minute was blissful. My technique was improving exponentially. Having arrived in the program as a transfer student, I was behind in the coursework. I carried a full course-load of dance and academic classes in hopes of catching up to my peers. Despite my overall contentment with Adelphi's dance program, I missed singing and acting. I explored brochures of other performing arts schools and discovered a school with a musical theater degree program. This particular school, The United States International University's School of Performing and Visual Arts, San Diego provided focused training in singing and was located in sunny California. That was it! I set out for the Golden State without realizing that I was using a "stepping stone approach" to my goals. The **vision** was now aligning with my dream, providing a pathway to my reality.

After only one year at Adelphi University as a dance major, life was changing. I spent the summer working feverishly for my father's home-improvement contractors business, and as a babysitter. I needed funds to purchase a plane ticket for my San Diego voyage. I continually checked trade papers for possible theater jobs, and was thrilled when I found an audition for tap dancers to appear at the closing ceremony of Miss Liberty. A total of 300 tap dancers were needed to dance behind the esteemed, Liza Minelli, who would belt out her trade mark version of *New York, New York*. The ceremony was scheduled to be televised and performed live at The Meadowlands in New Jersey on July 6th. How could I miss this opportunity? I took myself to the audition, and within one week, received word that I had won a dance spot. This news astounded me! I was not only slated to appear on national television, but I was also going to perform with Liza Minelli. The event was a learning experience. My family was excited beyond words, and my proud brother attended the live performance. I remember my father asked his friend to tape the broadcast on VHS. Watching the special on television was surreal; it was only on that occasion that it hit me; I was a performer. My introduction to the world of television, however, has been disillusioning. The consolation was meeting R Chuck Vinson, a friend and resource for years to come. The problem that television presented was its lack of authenticity. On TV, everything seemed glamorous, but the work require to make a shoot seem natural was disconcerting. The end product was fake. Television just wasn't for me.

At this point in my life, I began to realize that my ambition and choices were determining factors. They were the keys to my ability to live out my purpose. My desire was to be someone special and to impact the world in a meaningful way. There were sacrifices along the way, and I had to maintain focus. The Miss Liberty television special was exciting, yet it cost me a friendship. My childhood friends had been irritated that I could not attend a pre-planned Virginia Beach spring break vacation due to my commitment. Additionally, I had been accepted as an audition candidate for The United States International University's School of Performing and Visual Arts (San Diego) based on my initial application. With money for a plane ticket and a self-choreographed jazz dance routine to *Disco Inferno* by The Tramps, I was California-bound. Fearless, faith filled and ready to meet my destiny, I had to make this journey. A problem remained; I had booked a round trip ticket for a two week stay in California, yet knew no one in the state, had no place to stay, and had limited monetary funds. My mother sat me down to plan the trip. She had never traveled to California, so she was quite intimidated by the idea that I would be arriving there shortly. Armed with Triple A Auto club and a trip assistant representative, she phones the necessary sources and booked a safe Los Angeles hotel, close to Sunset Boulevard, for the duration of my stay. She helped me procure an Amtrak to enable my safe travels between San Diego and Los Angeles. Finally, she contacted a relative, my Aunt Louella, in Mira Loma, California to provide me with familial contact on the West Coast. My mother went above and beyond to make my trip successful. Her planning and care afforded me the support I needed, and an acceptance spot at The United States International University's School of Performing and Visual Arts (San Diego) was soon granted. Life was taking shape beautifully, and California dreaming was just beginning. DETERMINATION, AMBITION, DRIVE, being RELENTLESS, having VISION, and following my PASSION were essential to the fulfillment of my DREAM.

Chapter Two

New York to California & Back!

Somehow, I knew in the depths of my soul that I would live in California at some point in my life. Mainstream shows had influenced my view of the state prior to my visitation. *The Brady Bunch, Bewitched, The Partridge Family,* and *The Price is Right* created an impression that California was a cheerful place, where dreamers were welcomed and opportunities swirled. Of course, having trained as a musical theater performer, one would have assumed my goal was to arrive in New York City. Blocking out the noise from skeptics, I concentrated on the accomplishments that propelled me into that particular moment, I had encountered many obstacles along the way that precluded a traditional college graduation in four years. Because I had transferred schools twice, I found myself, once again, taking academic classes during my summer sessions to buttress my college credits. I took advantage of a trimester study abroad program with our sister school, The International University Europe in Bushey Watford,

England. This "once in a lifetime" experience enriched my life. Each week, our theater class traveled to London to attend a play or musical. We interacted with multi-cultural students and engaged in fencing classes from Bill Hobbs, one of the original *Three Musketeers.* It was crazy! For three months, we were vivacious college kids, partying every weekend at local discotheques. I still remember the "song du jour," *It Takes Two to Make a Thing Go Right* by Rapper Ra Base. The song sampled James Brown's distinctive raspy voice squawk. When the song filled the club, everyone rushed to the dance floor. As an American, I enjoyed the perks of traveling abroad. There was seldom a shortage of attention, dance partners or drinks. While I had a Navy boyfriend, Vic, back home in the states, I still met plenty of guys, both at school and in the club scene. A friendship with a young man, "Said," from Oman, a place in the Gulf of the Middle East that was unfamiliar to me, developed. "Said" and I shared intimate conversations. A highlight of our special time together occurred when he invited me to meet his family, including his mother and sister during his graduation ceremony. "Said" was a real life prince, studying international business at IUE. At the time, it didn't resonate just how much my world was changing. I was being exposed to people whose backgrounds were different from mine and, at times, attractively exotic. It was easy to be seduced by forces that might impede my dreams. During this time, I applied my **disciplinary** skills. Being far from my native United States, I realized the critical role that discipline and restraint played in my life. By listening, following the direction of my instructors, heeding the words of my parents and my **prayers,** I was able to navigate a path around distractions, toward my goals. As a young adult, it was easy to feel the false sense of security that new independence provides. Away from adult supervision, I could fall into a pattern of believing that I possessed all the answers. Fortunately, I relied on sage counsel from my parents and my inner prayer voice. **Wise counsel, sound advice,** my parents and going within (prayer) were my **structure** while abroad. Discipline!

Upon leaving London and returning to my California college campus, I resumed my private voice lessons with an adept instructor, Ms. Fran Bjornby. Bjornby's vocal tutelage helped me expand my singing abilities, and she helped me schedule additional voice sessions to expedite my progress. I would practice my songs in the private practice rooms constantly. On occasion, I practiced with a male piano major student, Eric. This young man had an astute ear and could play anything, as long as he could play by ear. He and I were part of the choral ensemble together, as well. He wrote and sang his own songs, so he was the logical choice to assist me with my first attempt at songwriting. He put a melody to the lyrics of a poem I had written. Before I knew it, we had collaborated and produced a legitimate song that I would perform with other school musicians, including my friend, Walter Emanuel Jones.

At the end of the third trimester at the university, performing arts' students endured juries, final exams for each performance major. Regretfully, I had not secured a role in any school production at the Oldtown Theater in downtown San Diego. As a result, I had to schedule my exams and performance evaluation with the director of our school, Mr. Jack Tygett. In an amazing stroke of good fortune, I was contacted by my only television connection, R Chuck Vinson. Vinson was the directing stage manager on the Cosby Show and was working on a pilot spin-off called *A Different World.* He contacted me to work on this pilot at KTLA Studios (Los

Angeles). The timing couldn't be more perfect! With the booking of a television pilot and a paycheck, my juries were excused. It was an automatic pass. I did, however, eventually reject Vinson's offer for an extra casting position. Finishing my degree and attaining a Bachelor of Fine Arts (BFA) was one of my life's highlights. I refused to turn my back on that final piece of my educational pursuits.

Within months, I had recognized a yearning to return to New York City. Life in California, though busy, was still lonely. There were few family members and friends, aside from my Aunt Louella in Mira Loma, surrounding me. I appreciated the experience of working on a television pilot; it had been surreal. The best choice I could make for my life, however, was to return to the love and support of my family in New York City. With help from my navy boyfriend, Vic, who refused to stand in the way of my ambition, I packed up my California life. My brother flew from New York to join me on the drive home. Together, we set out on the excursion home in my five-speed red Hyundai, complete with my two cats, Misty and Mindy. I bid California farewell and returned to "The Big Apple," ready to pound the pavement and start my theater career. I was finally prepared to **focus. STRUCTURE,** wise **COUNSEL,** sound **ADVICE, PRAYER, DISCIPLINE,** and **FOCUS,** sustained me on the road to my **DREAM.**

Chapter Three

Auditions

"Out of every 100 auditions you do, you may get one job." I could still hear Jack Tygett's wisdom from my days at the United States International University in San Diego. What could I do to beat these odds? Immediately, I faced the mirror and stripped down to my "birthday suit." What do people see when they look at me? I pondered that question and closed my eyes. Silence. As I opened my eyes, reflecting back was the image of a young woman. She was a thin, black female, with average height, and medium/light brown skin. I saw brown eyes, thick dark brown medium-length hair, long fingers and a one-dimpled smile. I looked closer. Am I pretty enough? Am I thin enough to catch a director's eye? Am I tall enough? Am I good enough? Audition questions pertaining to my worth flooded my mind. Stop! I had come this far; there was no turning me back. Determined to dress this image staring back in the mirror, I dove into my closet. In that moment of reflection, I resolved that "I" was my own product. No one would sell my image but "me." What would my product's name be? *MarQue Munday - Singer, Dancer, Actress, Model.* Done. How would I know where to market *MarQue*? I would subscribe to trade magazines, including *Backstage,* the weekly audition publication notice. At once, I was ready to tackle the task of landing a professional theater job in New York City.

Scouring *Backstage* fascinated me. There were copious shows listed in the audition section for musicals. I noticed many classic audition listings, *Carousel, My Fair Lady, 42nd Street, and Camelot.* Then, it leaped out from the page - *Dreamgirls!* Was I, in fact, dreaming? I carefully checked the listing to find this audition's time and location. Immediately, I recorded the information into my daily planner. How about the other auditions, I wondered? Might I attend these try outs, as well? If I was lucky, an ensemble role might be available for a black woman. I resolved to focus on my *Dreamgirls* audition. Surely, I would be "right" for some part in the black-based production. The *Dreamgirls* audition occurred in midtown Manhattan and was packed with desperate auditionees. Never in my lifetime had I encountered rows of women who looked like me. We were all the same "type," concentrated into one audition event. How would I make myself stand out? I focused on the task at hand, the audition. Afterwards, fate took over, and I received a call back. Upon completion of this return audition, I secured my first professional musical theater job. Director, Weyman Thompson had cast me in *Dreamgirls* at the Bridgeport Dinner Theater in Connecticut. Finally, I had achieved my own dream of performing professionally close to my home city.

As theater people will tell you, one job often opens the doors to another. By the time *Dreamgirls* had closed in Connecticut, I received an additional job offer. This time, I was cast in a touring production of *Faith Journey*. The director was Jessie Devour, and the show chronicled the life of Dr. Martin Luther King Jr. The production detailed the struggles African Americans had endured during the Civil Rights Movement. It consisted of a cast of six performers. We toured the eastern portion of the United States, from Boston to Alabama, and eventually returned to New York City. *Faith Journey* was staged sporadically for many years, while the production struggled to procure funding. In the interim, I was cast in another Bridgeport Dinner Theater production of *The Wiz.* This time, Thompson directed and starred in the musical. I was cast as an ensemble member. Already, I could consider myself a "working actor," having performed professionally in consecutive shows. My colleagues and fellow performers were incredible talents. Many of these gifted individuals, from my distant and recent past, were gaining accolades. Eric, for example, the piano major who had assisted me on my first song-writing endeavor in San Diego, hit stardom and became known as, Jamie Foxx. Walter, the other student collaborator from my San Diego days, became the fearless ZACK, the black Power Ranger who graciously wrote the foreword in this book. Other colleagues, such as Jerry Maple and Grace Young from *Faith Journey*, pursued successful directing, acting and singing careers. Another performer, Frederick Bruce Owens, launched a film and Broadway career with his performance onscreen in the movie, *Hitch,* and his role in the Broadway smash hit, *Smokey Joe's Cafe.* It was apparent now. Over the past years, I had aligned myself with gifted performers who enhanced my talent and made me a better singer, dancer and actor. Most of these former colleagues remain a part of my life to this day, and I am grateful for their contributions to my life.

Theater life in New York City had gotten off to a busy start. Performing opportunities had presented themselves consistently, and I no longer had to work temp jobs to supplement my income. **Consistent** work gave me confidence and a belief in my abilities. My audition formula was getting me **consistent** employment. Everything had fallen into place. As spring approached, I was on a break from a European musical tour with *Golden Musical of Broadway.* It was April, and Radio City Music Hall had announced auditions for *The Rockettes.* The opportunity created turbulence in my mind. Should I attend the audition? Was this audition a landmark moment in my life? Two years prior, I had missed the Radio City Rockettes audition because I had been gainfully employed. This time, I was back temping in the city, awaiting the return of our tour. There was no way I would miss the audition! On audition day, there were 900 Rockette hopefuls in attendance. The criteria for becoming a Rockette was: (1) possessing proficiency in ballet tap and jazz (2) measuring between 5' 5 1/2"" to 5' 9" and (3) being able to sing 16 bars from a musical selection. Boy, did I feel ready to compete for a coveted spot in this dance troupe line. If my memory serve me correctly, my audition number was #468.

When we arrived at Radio City, we were ushered into a long hallway for the measurement portion of the audition. Next, we were assembled into a line. This "line up" assessment was to determine each of our "types." "Typing" occurs when an audition panel views a candidate to ensure that she has the correct "look" for the role. At each of these two points in the process, women were cut from the audition. In my case, I passed both of these tests easily. The next phase of the audition involved a tap routine. My inner voice told me to relax and enjoy learning the dance. All my life, I had been tapping; it was second nature. Violet Holmes, a former Rockette who had risen in the organization as a choreographer, and her assistant taught a tap routine. I watched the choreography and listened to Violet intently. It was a lovely, stylistic piece that felt comfortable. With smooth steps and an elegant style, I executed the routine for the audition panel. We were asked to switch lines and repeat our dance, providing all dancers with a chance to view their performance in the mirror. Eventually, we were divided into groups of four to six dancers, with two staggered lines. Each group performed the routine twice, switching lines after completing the routine. The panel had clear views of every Rockette hopeful. We didn't have much time to impress our judges. It was imperative that we "sell it," and prove our competency and star quality now. I delivered clean, spirited routines both times during the audition. I knew in my heart I had "nailed it." After waiting for each group's completed dances, we were grouped into a kickline. This moment provided the most excitement. Here I was, in Radio City Music Hall's famed Rehearsal Room, and I was participating in a Rockette kickline. We were taught one of the Rockette's world famous "eye-high" kicking combinations. Could someone pinch me please? The kickline combination required strong technique and form to master. We were linked together, kicking in unison; however, no woman was allowed to touch the other's back. The kick line required concentration and precision. When we finished the kicking portion of the auction, we were instructed to leave the premises. In the event that the judge panel was interested in hiring us as a Rockette, we would receive a phone call offering a call back audition. We were encouraged to continue practicing the dance routines from the audition. When I arrived home, I immediately began practicing all of the choreography we had learned. To practice the kicks and ensure I didn't move from my designated position, I put a tape mark on the floor of my apartment in the most precarious spot I could find - the front of my glass wall unit. If I missed my mark, there would be an abundance of pain and mess. This gal meant business!

After several days, I received a call from Radio City Rockette Operations Manager, Melissa. She explained that the audition panel would like to see me for callbacks on a Thursday between 10 am and 1 pm. YEEEESSSS! I couldn't contain my joy! I repeated the times to Melissa and thanked her profusely. On that particular week, I was on work assignment. I needed to rearrange my schedule so I could leave at lunchtime. I figured I could work in the early morning and complete my callback by the early afternoon. I had been preparing the audition routines diligently. Since my temp agency assignment was in the city, I was able to bring my audition gear (my tap, jazz & ballet shoes; leotard & tights; headshot & resume; and sheet music) to work. The minutes ticked by slowly that morning. By 11 am, I had completed my temp work and left my job for the day. I headed up to Midtown and then to the 50th Street Station on the Number One train. Hurriedly, I made my way across Sixth Avenue and 51st Street to the Radio City Music Hall Stage Door. The door opened and all I could see were Rockette hopefuls pouring out of the cramped room. One red-lipped auditionee looked at me and said, "It's over. You missed it." My heart stopped. My eyes welled up. I turned to the Radio City doorman named, Bob. Bob said, "Hold on, I will call up to the Rehearsal Hall and see if anyone is still there." I stood in stillness, stunned by the news that I had missed this critical moment in my life. I watched gorgeous women filing out of an elevator and leaving through a doorway that leads to 51st Street. Bob interrupted my stillness. "Someone will be right down to get you." Taking a deep breath, I collected my nerves. As Melissa, the Rockette Operations Manager arrived to escort me to the Rehearsal Hall, I dug deep into my soul and decided, "I got this."

Still incredulous over my mistake about the audition time, I waited while Melissa and I rode the elevator to my destiny. The doors opened, and I was met by the Rockette Director, Bruce Michael. He expressed concern that I might have been injured or sick. I was humbled by his genuine worry about my well-being. As I entered the large Rehearsal Room, I apologized to the audition panel for my tardiness. Immediately, the audition began with Violet Holmes reviewing the dance combinations. I rushed to secure my tap shoes and unveil my audition outfit. We practiced the routines twice and, then, I was left on the floor to perform alone. After I completed my dances, I was asked to sing and undergo a taped interview. As the call back auction concluded, I thanked the panel for their understanding of my circumstances and gathered my belongings. Melissa accompanied me back to the elevator. When I arrived at the Stage Door exit area, Bob, the doorman, was still there. I thanked him with all my heart for his kindness. I emerged from Radio City onto the busy New York City sidewalk. I had done it. My heart pounded within my chest. It was now in God's hands.

Waiting for that call from Radio City was interminable. In the meantime, I had already returned to the European tour of a musical review for a six month contract. It was a non-union contract, which meant that living conditions could be less than desirable. We had to share rooms with fellow cast and crew members, and there was no per diem pay. Being young, traveling throughout Europe, and performing made the conditions bearable - even exhilarating. On one particular night, our touring company endured a long bus ride. It was frigid and late. We were exhausted, but hungry. I had acquired a few soup packets in my bag and needed hot water. One of the musicians from our production, Holger, looked pale and irritable. He was famished, so I offered him a soup packet. You would have thought I had offered him gold; he dropped his bags and sped to my room. He gulped down asparagus soup (I had never tried asparagus soup). The water remained tepid, so the soup tasted disgusting. But, this musician didn't mind. He ate with no complaints. Holger and I eventually dated for two years. It was a pleasant surprise to meet such a dear friend during this tour. Little did I realize, but my life was about to be changed forever. Within four months of the European tour and my new relationship with Holger, I received a message from my mother. Radio City Music Hall had called. Without hesitation, I phoned Bruce Michaels, the Rockette Director. Over the phone, he offered me a position as a Rockette in the Radio City Christmas

Spectacular. Rehearsals would begin on October 23, my birthday! I was scheduled to report to Radio City Music Hall for a costume fitting in seven days, exactly one week from our phone conversation. That night, I gave my notice to our tour Manager. My dream had arrived, and I had to follow it back home. I booked the first flight I could find and began my return to New York City.

Fate? Destiny? The imprint on my soul from childhood? My life's experiences had led to this moment. I had **accomplished** the three goals I had identified early in my life. I had become an actress on a television show, like Penny from *Goodtimes.* I had performed in my favorite musical, *Dreamgirls.* Finally, my grandest, sweetest childhood dream was now a reality. I was a Radio City Rockette. What odds had I beaten? Eventually, I would understand the significance of my Rockette selection as an African American dancer. Even the hurdles I had encountered, took on new meaning. The late callback to the Rockette audition had afforded me a unique experience, after all. Mr. George Lemoines, Radio City Music Hall's Historian had been present during my final callback. He managed to film my entire audition and presented me with a copy of my

Rockette callback when I began working in the Christmas show. That Rockette audition tape is a treasure that few Rockettes ever receive. **FATE, DESTINY, CONSISTENT, PREPARED, and ACCOMPLISH. BELIEVE** you will **ACHIEVE** and **RECEIVE** your extraordinary life of **PASSION** and purpose.

Chapter Four

8 Years a Radio City Music Hall Rockette

In my entire performing career, no feeling has ever rivaled the excitement of being hired as a Radio City Rockette. Becoming part of this elite, legendary group held significance far beyond dance steps and fancy costumes. My acceptance, as an African American woman, into the Rockette organization was unique. Prior to my hiring, there had only been one other African American Rockette at Radio City Music Hall in American history. This fact astounded me. How could it be true that my beloved Rockette organization had only managed to hire two African American ladies since 1932? The year of my hire was 1992 and, as I delved into Radio City's history, the truth emerged. The first woman hired to represent the African American culture as a Rockette was a woman named Jennifer. She had been hired in 1988. Hadn't the Civil Rights Movement occurred in the 1960s? Why was Radio City's representation of diversity in its Rockette line lacking? As ground breakers in the Rockette organization, there was a determination to represent ourselves and our respective history with dignity, class, and adeptness.

Dancing as a Rockette required practice and a strong work ethic. We rehearsed six days a week, from ten in the morning until five in the afternoon. The rehearsals were intimidating and expectations for our mastery of dances were high. Not only were the dance steps demanding, but there were also endless rules for Rockette etiquette and "sisterhood," that we needed to follow. I wasn't used to a corporate approach in the artistic world and, consequently, felt like a "fish out of water." The incoming newbies, including myself, consisted of nine women. The physical fatigue, along with the pressure to learn production numbers in rapid increments, made me consider quitting during the first weeks of rehearsals. The best advice I received came from a lovely dancer, Mary. She said, "Don't let anyone take your job from you. This is *your* job. You earned it!" I was instantly reminded of "the odds" I had always encountered in show biz. Nowhere had these odds been more amplified than in the Rockette kick line. Here I stood, in a line of primarily Caucasian women. Where were the Rockettes who represented minority groups?

All I could find were two black women, including myself, one Asian woman, and one Puerto Rican woman. Four of us represented "the odds," and we stood proudly. No negative remarks or eye rolls would diminish our experience. I couldn't help but remember Bernadette, the beautiful, talented dancer from my childhood. She had possessed unparalleled talent, yet had been denied the opportunity to become a Rockette. So I had to **stand**. I represented the hopes and dreams of African American women, and nothing would stop me from basking in that glory.

The year I became a Rockette, the New York Times published an article that referred to the Rockettes as still being all Caucasian. The four women representing minority groups were fair, light skinned, and the line, consequently, appeared unified. Our African American presence in the Rockette line proved Russell Markert's claim that dark skin tones would ruin his trademark unison precision look. Markert had instituted a policy whereby Caucasian Rockettes could not become sun-tanned. With the advent of minorities in the Rockette troupe, I was on the cusp of truly kicking the odds. Change had arrived and nothing would stop the momentum.

As I settled into life as a Rockette, I began to set a personal goal. I told myself, I will be a Rockette for five years. My longest show experience had been my six month European contract. Five years as a Rockette meant performing in the two seasonal productions, *The Radio City Christmas Spectacular* and *The Radio City Easter Extravaganza.* I soon learned that Rockettes had more performing opportunities than most dance troupes. I availed myself of many additional Rockette appearances including performances in the Macy's Day Parade, The Rockefeller Christmas Tree Lighting, The David Letterman Show, the FAO Schwartz Rockette Barbie Doll Launch, The Peter Allen Benefit, Los Angeles, and The Memphis Graceland and ELVIS event. I proudly served as a tour guide Rockette for Radio City Music Hall. Meeting tourists from around the world thrilled me, and I loved sharing information about the history of the Radio City Rockettes, as well as, posing for tourist photographs. One of the most interesting Rockette opportunities arrived when I joined The Great Radio City 60th Anniversary Spectacular in Las Vegas. This production had originated as a national touring show and had found a permanent home at the Flamingo

Hilton Hotel in Las Vegas. Being a Radio City Rockette could be a career all by itself with the endless performance opportunities.

Each Rockette show involved similar choreographic routines and a variety of kick lines. We had a repertoire of kicking styles ranging from flick kicks to our famous eye-high kicks. New choreographers always presented a challenge to the Rockettes. Precision dancing required attention to detail and choreography that used lines, angles and sharp movements. Precision choreography was difficult to achieve with flowing, soft movements. Rockette choreographers faced great challenges. I had the good fortune of working with many of the Rockettes' legendary choreographers, including Violet Holmes, Scott Salmon, Bobby Longbottom, John Diertich, Maurice Hines, and David Scala. Each of these creators made a distinct mark on the choreography of the Rockettes.

Over the years, many favorite Rockette moments stand out. During my first year as a Rockette, the Christmas show added the *Rag Doll* number, created by Scott Salmon. It required precision tapping and teamwork to create the illusion of rag dolls dancing in a toy factory. Today, this *Rag Doll* number still appears in the Christmas show and was recently modified for a new generation of Rockettes. Another favorite Rockette number was *Christmas in New York*, choreographed by Violet Holmes. I was excited to debut this number, which featured a kick line to *White Christmas* and a live ice skating exhibition on The Great Stage. I remember fondly the "green number," *Rocking Around the Christmas Tree* by Bobby Longbottom. In that number, we entered the stage flapping through a massive Christmas tree. I loved the *Wreath Number* where we danced on the Radio City passerelle, a semicircular ramp that extends from the stage in front of the orchestra pit. In this routine, the audience was barely a foot in front of us. It was special seeing the crowds so close as we danced and kicked. I loved the *Carol of Bells*, a classic Rockette routine that culminated with each Rockette playing an xylophone on another dancer's back.

The Radio City Easter Extravaganza introduced me to new talents, including the late tap dancer, Greg Burg, and Linda Haberman, the show's creator and choreographer. I was honored to participate in the Easter show's last performance of the Rockette's famed, *Dancing in the Dark* routine. I was ecstatic over the opportunity I received to perform in the Macy's Day Parade and the Tree Lighting Ceremony at Rockefeller Center. I had grown up watching these events on television. It was a dream to appear on television in New York City during the holiday season. The prestige of the Rockettes gave me status as an elite dancer. The roar of the audience let me know, without a doubt, that I was Rockette royalty.

In 1995, I joined the Great Radio City Spectacular in Las Vegas, shortly after it arrived at The Flamingo Hilton hotel. Susan Anton co-starred with the Rockettes in this production, and working with her solidified my desire to become a singer and headliner in the future. The Vegas Rockette show displayed entertainment that was unfamiliar. Jugglers, puppeteers, dog acts, ventriloquists, magicians, hypnotists, illusionists, as well as comedians, adagio dance teams, and singers performed alongside the Rockettes. Our signature dance numbers from this show included *Bolero, The Gold & Silver Fan Dance, The Parade of the Wooden*

Soldiers and our famous *Dancing in Diamonds* piece, with costumes designed by Bob Mackey. This *Dancing in Diamonds* routine included over 100 kicks. Eventually, Maurice Hines co-starred in our show. He also choreographed one of the last Rockette numbers I danced, *Luck be a Lady.* My experience in the Las Vegas show wasn't always easy. Although the year-round performance schedule was lucrative, my ambition to create art and to sing gave way to frustration. I bounced in and out of the Vegas company, ending the show's run in July of 2000 as a swing performer, a rewarding and challenging Rockette position. By the show's final curtain, I had appeared with numerous celebrities, including Rip Taylor, Luther Vandross, Paige O'Hara, Mel B, David Cassidy, Barbara Eden, Florence Henderson, Nell Carter, Barry White, and Liza Minelli. The closing of the show also represented the ending of my Rockette experience. I had remained a Rockette for eight incredible years, surpassing my original goal of five years. Realizing that the number eight represents new beginnings, I decided to embrace a fresh start. With grace, I closed this chapter of my life and resolved to move on.

While in the Las Vegas Rockette show, my life changed forever when I met and married a jazz tenor saxophone player, Mark Vega. Mark and I eventually welcomed a son, Markus. The challenges of showbiz life and the music industry presented obstacles that Mark and I could not overcome. Twice, we tried to hold our marriage together. Regretfully, our efforts failed. Today, twenty years later, Mark and I are grandparents. We love our son and are part of his life, as he navigates young adulthood and parenting.

Chapter Five

The Odds

As a teenager, nothing could have convinced me that I would one day become a world famous Radio City Music Hall Rockette. As a three year old, I dreamed of this life, but as a teenager, I knew my reality would be different. The social climate of my New York world dictated a hierarchy. I knew my place in this racial and economic class structure. I knew my aunties were maids for the doctors on "the hill." My father, I understood, was a butler for the white 'Markey' family. It had been easier to believe that my future held endless possibilities when I was a child. The older I became, the more I sensed that there were external limits. My other fear was that I might hold internal limits too.

By the time I reached high school at Staten Island Academy, I accepted that "the odds were stacked against me." My spirit still bubbled out of me; I was wide-eyed, ambitious and ready to conquer the world. I just needed a plan to become a performer and escape this cruel world of racial prejudice. Ironically, the theme of my life, as I became a performer, was fitting the part. I constantly compared myself to a type. Am I the right color, height, weight, skin tone? I racially profiled myself! My knowledge of the struggle for civil rights was also limited. In our history classes, we studied European history. Seldom was there American or Black history mentioned. Martin Luther King Jr's birthday was celebrated with a day off from school. Black history just didn't seem worth researching. If my teachers and school were not concerned with these topics, why should I care? The primary concern of my high school was to prepare its students for college. Preparing us for life appeared to be secondary.

Why was life plagued with race issues? Why couldn't I pursue a person or career that I loved, regardless of the color of my skin? Why were adults and teachers afraid to discuss the ugly history of inequality so we might learn from our mistakes? Had I created **limits** for myself or was I searching for the **freedom** to participate in life as an **aspiring** African American? Dancing gave me the sensation of freedom and resolution from the conflicts and questions that life presented. By building on my past experiences, I could change my **future.** Nothing bound me to the past. I could control my own destiny. I wasn't going to wait anymore, or let society see me as a marginalized person. I was finally prepared to live.

Kicking the Odds

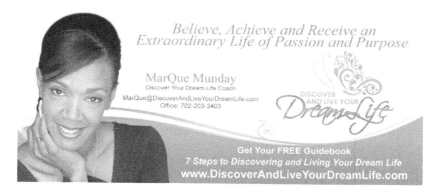

Believe, Achieve and Receive an Extraordinary Life of Passion and Purpose

MarQue Munday
Discover Your Dream Life Coach
MarQue@DiscoverAndLiveYourDreamLife.com
Office: 702-203-3403

DISCOVER
AND LIVE YOUR
Dream Life

Get Your FREE Guidebook
7 Steps to Discovering and Living Your Dream Life
www.DiscoverAndLiveYourDreamLife.com

"Discover and Live Your Dream Life"

So, right now grab a piece of paper or turn to the next blank page and write down all the DREAMS, GOALS, DESIRES, ASPIRATIONS, WISHES, PASSIONS, INTERESTS ETC... that you have and can think of. Your destiny awaits you kicking out of the box, *Kicking the Odds*, and this is just the place to get started. Once you see your dreams/ goals/ desires written down, say them aloud, so <u>You</u> can hear them. An example, I want to be a <u>lawyer</u>, I would <u>love to travel the world</u>, whatever it is. Once you see it and hear it, your vision will grab what is already imprinted inside of you and begin to universally align you with opportunities that will draw you in that direction. This may not happen over night, so post your list where you can see it daily upon waking and going to sleep. You can even make a vision board with picture illustrations of your dreams, goals, desires etc...

You must know without a shadow of a doubt that it is never to late to **Discover and Live Your Dream Life!** I encourage you to use my saying below, inserting who you are... This (who or what you are or want to be) _____'s Dream... and post it with your list/vision board and affirmation.

Example/Affirmation: This **DANCERS** Dream! 'I Believe, I can Achieve, and will Receive an extraordinary life of Passion and Purpose - With no **LIMITS**, I continue to **ASPIRE** to be all that I was uniquely created for, walking in my **FREEDOM** and Kicking all ODDS!'

You can be ALL that you were uniquely created and purposed to be in this life!

DREAMS, GOALS, DESIRES, ASPIRATIONS, WISHES, PASSIONS, INTERESTS ETC...

Photo Gallery

My Rockette Debut at RCMH 1992

My family: Parents - Daniel & Shirley Smith

Brother – David D. Smith, Aunt – Genevieve Shirell,

Sister in law – Kathleen Smith, Nephew – David D

Smith Jr. & God Son – Leon Joseph Pratt

MarQue's 1992 vision board photo's

performing as a Singer on RCMH Stage

Rockette 'MarQue Munday' doing Tours @RCMH

MarQue & Maurice Hines

Liza Minelli & MarQue

MarQue & Bruce Springsteen

Staten Island Advance Newspaper Article featuring their very own Staten Island Rockette – MarQue Munday

RCMH Mall Show

RCMH Christmas Spectacular – Dressing Room

MarQue Munday & Walter Jones

RCHM Newspaper Promo – Christmas Spectacular w/MarQue as Wooden Soldier

RCMH Easter Extravaganza

74

60th Anniversary Spectacular - LV Rockettes

Celebrating 100 Shows - Flamingo Las Vegas

Liberace Museum

Rockette's w/Wayne Newton

Rockettes –American Heart Association

Rockettes w/Marine Corp Reserve

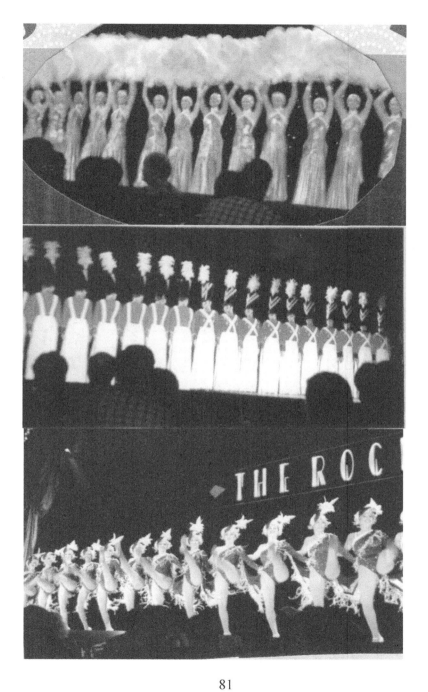

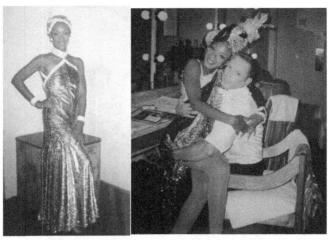

Book Cover Photo – Courteousy of Gina Giacinto-Simms

82

Rockettes w/Charlie Daniels

Rockettes w/Clint Black

Rockette's w/Florence Henderson (Brady Bunch Mom)

83

Rockettes w/Florence Henderson & Rip Taylor Co-Starring in the 60th Anniversary Spectacular

Rockette's w/Barbara Eden (I Dream of Jeannie)

Rockette's w/Mel B (Spice Girls)

Rockette w/Co-Star Maurice Hines
60th Anniversary Spectacular

MarQue in Rockette Showgirl Costume

60th Anniversary Spectacular Cast – Flamingo Hilton

90th Rockette Reunion RCHM
Rockettes

Rockette 1992 & Rockette 2015

Large Reh Hall RCMH @ 90th Reunion

90th Rockette Reunion Gala
Rockette Producer Bruce Michaels hired MarQue

Former Rockette Joanne Rush in
KICK: "It's Not How High, Its How Strong!"

Former Rockette Wendy Walker
@ her Show – "Suburban Showgirl"

Rockettes @ Good Morning America

(featuring Josh Groban)

Post Rockette Publicity
Daily Edition Sydney AUS Interview 2016

Oct 2016 I was interviewed on 'Daily Edition' an Australian afternoon talk show and referred to as 'Rockette Royalty' - who would have ever known?

Kicking 1 Up for Daily Edition Hosts Tom Williams & Sally Obermeder

Post Rockette Traditional Crowning – LV

Marque's Show &
After Party Crowning!

Former Rockette MarQue Munday
"Colors of a Dream"

Glossary of Key Words for SUCCESS:

This glossary has been created to encourage you as well as define what the words mean; knowledge, and continued growth are keys to your success.
Cambridge English Dictionary, Merriam-Webster Dictionary online, definitions at Google and dictionary.com

ACCOMPLISH - Achieve or complete successfully. To succeed in doing something. To finish something successfully or achieve something.

ACHIEVE - Read or attain a desired objective, level, or result by effort, skill, or courage. To succeed in finishing something or reaching an aim, especially after planning and working to make it happen. To carry out successfully.

ADVISE - Offer suggestions about the best course of action to someone. To give an opinion or suggestion to someone about what should be done. To give someone advise.

AMBITION - A strong desire to do or to achieve something, typically requiring determination and hard work. Desire to achieve a particular end. A strong wish to achieve something.

ASPIRE - Direct one's hopes or ambitions toward achieving something. To seek to attain or accomplish a particular goal. To have a strong hope or wish to have something.

BELIEVE - Accept something as true, feel sure of the truth. To have confidence in the truth, the existence, or reliability of something although without absolute proof that one is right in doing so. To have a firm religious faith. O accept something as true, genuine, or real. To think that something is true, correct, or real.

CHOICES - An art of selecting or making a decision when faced with two or more possibilities. The act of choosing. The act of picking or deciding between two or more possibilities. The act or an instance of choosing or selecting. The opportunity or power of choosing.

CONSEQUENCES - A result or effect of an action or condition. Importance or relevance. An act or instance of following something as an effect, result, or outcome.

CONSISTENTLY - In every case or on every occasion; invariably. In a fair and impartial way. Constantly adhering to the same principles, course, form, a consistent component. Marked by harmony, regularity, or steady continuity : free from variation or contradiction a consistent style. Being in agreement with itself; coherent and uniform.

CONTROL - The power to influence or direct people's behavior or the course of events. Determined the behavior or supervisor the running of. To check, limit, curb, or regulate; restrain. Manufacturing: device or mechanism installed or instituted to guide or regulate the activities or operation of an apparatus, machine, person, or system.

COUNSEL - Advice, especially that given formally. Advice given to someone. Advice, opinion or instruction given in directing the judgment or conduct of another. To give advice, especially on social or personal problems.

DANCE - Move rhythmically to music, typically following a set sequence of steps. A series of movements that match the speed and rhythm of a piece of music. And active staffing or moving through a series of movements usually in time to music. To move once feet or body, or both, rhythmically in a pattern of steps especially to the accompaniment of music.

DECISIONS - A conclusion or resolution reached after consideration. The action or process of deciding something or of resolving a question. A choice that you make about something after thinking about it: the result of deciding. A choice made between alternative courses of action in a situation of uncertainty.

DESTINY - The events that will necessarily happen to a particular person or thing in the future. The hidden power believe to control what will happen in the future; feet. Something to which a person or thing is destined: something that is to happen or has happened to a particular person or thing; lot of fortune. The predetermined, usually in evitable or irresistible, course of events. Your future or the pre-ordained path of your life.

DETERMINATION - Firmness of purpose resoluteness. The process of establishing something exactly, typically by calculation or research. A quality that makes you continue trying to do or chief something that is difficult. The active finding out or calculating something. The act of officially deciding something. The act of coming to a decision or a fixing or settling a purpose. The ability to continue trying to do something, even if it is difficult.

DISCIPLINE - Practice of training people to obey rules or a code of behavior, using punishment to correct disobedience . A branch of knowledge, typically one studied in higher education. Control that is gained by requiring that rules or orders be obeyed and punishing bad behavior. The suppression of base desires, and is usually understood to be synonymous with self-control, restraint and control.

DREAM - Dream series of thoughts, images, and sensations occurring in a person's mind during sleep. Contemplate the possibility of doing something or that something might be the case. A series of thoughts, visions, or feelings that happened during sleep. And idea or vision that is created in your imagination and that is not real. Something that you have wanted very much to do, be, or have for a long time. A series of images, ideas, emotions, and sensations occurring in voluntarily in the mind during certain stages of sleep.

DRIVE - Operate and control the direction and speed of a motor vehicle. Propel or carry along by force in a specified direction. And innate, biologically determined urge to attain a goal or satisfy a need. And organized effort to achieve a goal or fundraising drive.

FATE - The development of events beyond a person's control, regarded as determined by a supernatural power. To be destined to happen, turn out, or act in a particular way. The universal principle or ultimate agency by which the order of things is presumably prescribed; the decree cause of events; time. That which is in evitable he determined; destiny. The will or principal or determining caused by which things in general I believed to come to be as they are or events to happen as they do; destiny. What happens to a particular person or thing, especially something final or negative, such as death or defeat.

FREEDOM - The power or right to act, speak, or think as one wants without hindrance or restraint. The state of not being imprisoned or enslaved. The quality or state of being free: as a: the absence of necessity, coercion, or constraint in choice or action. Liberation from slavery or restraint or from the power of another. The quality or state of being exempt or released from something onerous. The state of being free or at liberty rather than in confinement or under physical restraint.

FOCUS - The center of interest or activity. The state or quality of having or producing clear visual definition. Pay particular attention to. A septic that is being discussed or studied. The subject on which peoples attention is focused. A main purpose or interest. A center point, as of attraction, attention, or activity.

HONESTY - Good and truthful. Not lying, stealing, or cheating. Showing or suggesting a good and truthful character. Not hiding the truth about someone or something. Honorable in principles, intentions, and action; up right and fair. Not meant to deceive someone. The quality or fact of being honest; uprightness and fairness.

INTEGRITY - The quality of being honest and having strong moral principles; moral rightness. The state of being full and undivided. Firm adherence to a code of especially moral or artistic valuables. Incorruptibility. An unimpaired condition. Soundness. Adherence to moral and ethical principles; soundness of moral character; honesty. The state of being a whole, entire, or undiminished.

LIMITS - A point or level beyond which something does not or may not extend or pass. A restriction on the size or amount of something permissible or possible. A point beyond which it is not possible to go.

ODDS - The ratio between the amounts staked by the parties to a bet, based on the expected probability either way. The chances or likelihood of something happening for being the case. Superiority in strength, power, or resources; advantage. The possibility that something will happen. The chance that one thing will happen instead of a different thing. Conditions that make it difficult for something to happen. Two numbers that show how much a person can win by betting a certain amount of money. The probability that something is so, will occur, or is more likely to occur then something else.

PASSION - Strong and barely controllable emotion. A strong feeling of enthusiasm or excitement for something or about doing something. A strong feeling that causes you to act in a dangerous way. A strong sexual or romantic feelings for someone. Any powerful or compelling emotion or feeling, as love or hate. A strong or extravagant fondness, enthusiasm, or desire for anything. Having, compelled by, or ruled by intense emotion was strong feeling fervid.

PERSEVERANCE - Steadfastness in doing something despite difficulty or delay in achieving success. Continued effort to do or achieve something despite difficulties, failure, or opposition. The action or condition or an instance of persevering steadfastness. Not giving up.

PRAYER - A salad request for help or expression of things addressed to God or an object of worship. And Ernest hope or wish. A religious service especially a regular one at which people gather in order to pray together. A devout petition to God or an object of worship. A spiritual communion with God or an object of worship, as in supplication, Thanksgiving, adoration, or confession. The act or practice of praying to God or an object of worship. Conversation with God; the intercourse of the soul with God, not in contemplation or meditation, but in direct address to him. And address (as a petition) to God or a God in word for thought said a prayer for the success of the voyage. A set order of words used in praying. And earnest request or wish.

PREJUDICE - Preconceived opinion that is not based on reason or actual experience. Harm or injury that results or may result from some action or judgment. And unfavorable opinion or feeling formed before hand or without knowledge, thought, or reason. Any preconceived opinion or feeling, either favorable or unfavorable. Unreasonable feelings, opinions, or attitudes, especially of a hostile nature, regarding an ethnic, racial, social or religious group. Preconceived judgment or opinion. An adverse opinion or leaning formed without just grounds or before sufficient knowledge. An instance of such judgment or opinion. An irrational attitude of hostility directed against an individual, group, a race, or their supposed characteristics.

PREPARED - Make (something) ready for use or consideration. Properly expectant, organized or equipped. Ready. To put in proper condition or readiness. Made at an earlier time for later use. Made ready in advance. Ready for something. In a suitable condition for some purpose or activity. Willing to do something. To make (someone or something) ready for some activity, purpose, use, etc. Ready to deal with a situation.

PURPOSE - The reason for which something is done or created or for which something exists. Have as one's intention or objective. The reason why something is done or used. The aim or intention of something. The feeling of being determined to do or achieve something. The aim or goal of a person. What a person is trying to do, become, etc. The reason for which anything is done, created, or exists. A fixed design, outcome, or idea, that is the object of an action or other effort. Fixed intention in doing something; determination.

RECEIVE - Be given, presented with four paid. Suffer, experience, or be subject to. To get Orby given (something). To react to (something) in a space specified way. To welcome (someone) in usually a formal way. To take into one's position (something offered or delivered). To have (something) bestowed, conferred, etc.

RELENTLESS - Oppressively consistent, incessant. Harsh or inflexible. Showing or promising no abatement of severity, intensity, strength, or pace. Unyieldingly severe, strict, or harsh. Unceasingly intense. Continuing in a severe or extreme way. Unyielding in severity or strictness. Steady and persistent, unremitting.

RESPONSIBILITY - The state or fact of having a duty to deal with something or of having control over someone. The state or fact of being accountable or to blame for something. The opportunity or ability to act independently and make decisions without authorization. The state of being the person who caused something to happen. A duty or task that you are required or expected to do. Something that you should do because it is morally right, legally required etc. The state or fact of being responsible, answerable, or accountable for something within one's power, control or management.

STAND - Have or maintain an upright position, supported by one's feet. (Of an object, building, or settlement) be situated in a particular place or position. An attitude toward a particular issue, a position taken in an argument. A place where, or an object on which, someone or something stands, sits or rest, in particular. To be in or take an upright position on the feet Stand for the pledge. To take up or stay in a specified position or condition Stand aside. The judges stood firm. To rest, remain, or set in and usually vertical position.

STRUCTURE - The arrangement of and relations between the parts or elements of something complex. Construct or arrange according to a plan; given a pattern or organization to. The way that something is built, arranged, or organized. The way that a group of people are organized. Something (such as a house, tower, bridge) that is built by putting parts together and that usually stands on its own. Mode of building, construction, or organization; arrangement of parts, elements, or constituents.

TRUST - The quality or state of being true. That which is true or in accordance with the fact or reality. A fact or belief that is accepted as true. The real facts about something. The things that are true. The quality or state of being true. A statement or idea that is true or accepted as true. Conformity with fact or reality, verity. A verified or indisputable fact, proposition, principal, or the like.

VISION - The faculty or state of being able to see. An experience of seeing something or something in a dream or trance, or as a supernatural apparition. The ability to see. Site or eyesight. Something that you imagine. A picture that you see in your mind. Something that you see or dream especially as part of a religious or supernatural experience. I mystical or religious experience of seeing some supernatural events, person, exit. And aspirational description of what an organization would like to achieve or accomplish in the mid term or long-term future.

My friend, Walter, and I

In Perth Australia we reconnected after 20 years –
both doing gigs miles away from home. We
promised to stay in touch.

Hanging out w/the family in California after
returning home from Australia.

Thanks Walter, you're a cherished friend, and I'm
so glad we met in college, stayed focused on our
"Dreams" and are still down to earth.
Blessings, Love & continued success to you!

The Many M's of Me – Finally I AM Free
By MarQue

She had it going on! Beautiful, successful, ambitious, motivated, strong, responsible, dependable, trust worthy, loving, caring, Christian, mother, wife, entrepreneur, and alone. What? Really... She had worked hard for many years building the empire she would leave as her legacy. She found biblical women to model herself after and validate her drive and continuous work ethic. She seemed like a machine churning out projects and products that should or would sustain her and her family financially.

Her constant motivation was turning dreams into reality and she wasn't afraid to put the necessary work in. She often worked so hard and furiously at her projects that time and people slipped by without her noticing. If she could plug you in for a quick appointment or meeting she would run in, get or give the necessary information, occasionally spend a minute chatting and off with a dash to her next appointment she went.

When she realized what had happened to her life, it was almost too late. Her son was a junior in high school and her husband, whom she loved desperately had gone...

My First Piano Lesson Book

By MarQue Smith

Non-Profit 501 C 3 - 2004

Music Department

Prepared by MarQue Smith

Update 9/2014

2nd Update 6/2016

A Musical foundation... Our first milestone will consist of practical knowledge of the instrument and basic technical execution of theory: Note identification on the piano, major scales and fingering. Second we will identify the musical notes, values and rhythm. And finally we learn the staff, reading, writing and notation. As we learn these basic's we will enjoy singing, clapping and playing the rhythm. Experience the joy of music.

W.I.T.N.E.S.S "Performing Arts Dance"

Walk In The NEW Testament Experiencing Spirit and Scripture
- by Ms. MarQue

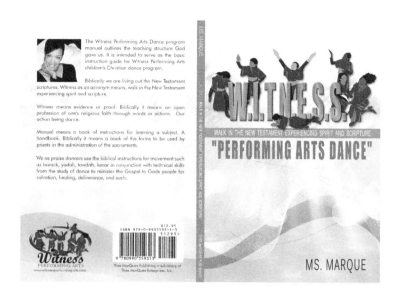

The Witness Performing Arts Dance program manual outlines the teaching structure God gave us. It is intended to serve as the basic instruction guide for Witness Performing Arts children's Christian dance program.

Biblically we are living out the New Testament scriptures. Witness as an acronym means, walk in the New Testament experiencing spirit and scripture.

Witness means evidence or proof. Biblically it means an open profession of one's religious faith through words or actions; Our action being dance.

115

Manual means a book of instructions for learning a subject. A handbook. Biblically it means a book of the forms to be used by priests in the administration of the sacraments.

We as praise dancers use the biblical instructions for movement such as barack, yadah, towdah, karar in conjunction with technical skills from the study of dance to minister the Gospel to Gods people for salvation, healing, deliverance, and such.

Training For The Worship Arts Technician
A Technician of Worship
- by MarQue

I had to ask God to reveal my calling with clarity because
He has given me many gifts. I needed His direction to put
things in order.

The first process He began was training me in different
areas and building my discipline. Becoming a performing
artist seemed natural to me because I started dancing at the
age of 3. So by the time I was ready for college it just
seemed obvious that I would be a dancer. However to my
parents and friends that wasn't a stable career choice, it was
an activity or hobby. My thought was, why would I spend
so much time and money doing something, learning
something, trying to perfect something that I would never
use again? I had been dancing for all but 3 years of my life

- it was like breathing to me. So I went to college for dance and then transferred to be a musical theatre major. Now I had taken piano lessons starting at age 8, so I could read music and play at a basic level and I started singing at the age of 12. The only area left was Drama which was covered in college and Fitness which seemed to fall right in line. During college I worked part-time at Jack-la-lane as a aerobics instructor and shortly after my professional dance career I transitions and became a certified Pilates Instructor.

Training is the staple in my life. The scripture says, train up a child in the way they should go... So I am a trainer. A technician in the Arts and Fitness field for Christ.

Training to Reign

- by Reign Dance Company

Ms MarQue had the honor and pleasure of being the technical trainer for Reign Dance Company, who released their first Dance Ministry book in April 2014. Transform your Worship Arts Ministry forever! Let Reign Dance Company share their testimonies of how a Christian dance company succeeds with a team-based leadership approach. If you desire to launch a dynamic church dance ministry, a community-based arts organization or a global arts outreach mission team, Training to Reign will provide the steps needed to triumph. Begin your kingdom training session today!

Friendly Tips For Flying Trips
By MarQue

This little book of tips and HINTS for flying is just that, "LITTLE"! Although it is packed full of all kinds of information, all the areas and topic's covered can be expanded into books of their own. Use this book along with our website and the facebook page to read stories about flying and get general information regarding the flying industry. You should always refer to your carrier for specific and detailed information about your particular itinerary.

It is my sincere desire that you have a Safe, Happy and Fun Flying experience...

Welcome Aboard!

7 Steps to Discovering and Living Your Dream Life
By MarQue Munday

You can live your 'Dream Life'. If you think that sounds to good to be true, that is exactly why I'm willing to walk with you and show you how you can 'Discover and Live Your Dream Life'. My name is MarQue and if you will allow me, I will be your 'Dream Life Coach'. When something sounds to good to be true, we dismiss it and continue doing the same things we have been doing - grunting, complaining and wishing there was a better way. Well, now there is... 7 Steps to Discovering and Living Your Dream Life. Together we will walk through these 7 Steps that provide a practical application method for you to live your dream life. This is not a magical - "poof there it is". These steps will take time and effort. So, if you truly want to live an extraordinary life of passion and purpose lets get started because Your Dream Life is just Ahead!

If you can Believe, you can Achieve and you will Receive.

AUTHOR'S BIO

MarQue strives to reach the highest level of excellence in her career field possible, maintaining a humble and respectful stature. Scripture 2 Tim 2:15 "Study to shew thyself approved unto God, a workman that needeth not be ashamed, rightly dividing the word of truth". She is a Rockette Alumnae Radio City Music Hall, graduated from the United States International University (now Alliant Univ.) in San Diego, CA - with a Bachelor's degree in Fine Arts (Musical theatre - Singer/Dancer/Actress). Originally from Staten Island, New York, MarQue was relocated to Las Vegas with The Rockettes in 1995 to perform at the Flamingo.

In 1999 she was called to the inaugural cruise of the Disney Wonder Cruise Ship, and was the female lead singer on the ship's first run at sea, from Venice, Italy to Cape Canaveral, Florida. She has headlined on both the Venus Pacific and Asuka Japanese Cruise ships. MarQue is the Founder/Director/Instructor/and Choreographer for Witness Performing Arts, Inc., a non-profit performing arts program, now online mentorship that teaches dance to students ages 3 – 12 and Pilates Christinexercise sessions based on Christian scriptures. MarQue was a member of and Dance Technical Trainer for Reign Dance Company directed by Rekesha Pittman. As President/CEO of Thee MarQuee Enterprises, Inc. MarQue still performs, honing her gifts and talents in Music, Dance, Singing & Acting. MarQue has performed or appeared with legends Liza Minelli, Jeffrey Osborne, Rip Taylor, Maurice Hines, Nell Carter, Susan Anton, Luther Vandross, Chaka Kahn, Lou Rawls, Joshua Redman, Diana Ross, Barry White, Marilyn McCoo, Billy Davis Jr. and others. She toured as a Marvelette, the legendary Motown group, and has performed nationally as well as internationally on television, radio, cable, off-Broadway and film. Recently she starred in a NEW original musical play "When A Woman Loves", written and directed by Vivian Ross, and she was a feature in Motown Extreme Tribute show in Las Vegas. Locally MarQue performed in the Blues School House program at the House of Blues, Las Vegas Nevada. As a certified Pilates Instructor and Trainer, MarQue provided strength and conditioning for the Artists at Cirque du Soleil, Las Vegas and she has her own series of Pilates workout DVD's (w/a feature in Pilates Style Magazine).

She debuted as a Contemporary Christian singer with her CD titled "Partner In Life". She has also released a line of praise dancewear for children called "Praise Dance Multiples" and launched CHRISTINEXERCISE Magazine – Interviews of everyday people and how they "Live a life pleasing and acceptable to Christ." MarQue has choreographed for Polish Triplet Violinists "Alizma", Male Tribute group "Spectrum" and Female Tribute group "Radiance" whom she also tours with. On her own she calls her Pop/Jazz Band **"No Limit"**.

She is honored to answer the call of being an Author under the instruction of Pastor Rekesha Pittman and The Eagles International Authors Institute. As an Arts Technician she has made the transition to Independent certified Coach/Teacher and Speaker - John Maxwell Team, she launched her brand "Discover and Live Your Dream Life" (mentor Debbie Allen, Branding Expert) and JT Foxx Millionaire Underdog. Look for her new TV-Show *Dream Life* (Xperienc On Demand). MarQue is also a Mother, Glam – Ma, flight attendant and dedicated Worshiper using all her gifts and talents for the glory of God. She loves The Lord and truly believes ALL things are possible for him who believes (Mark 9:23).

Discover and Live Your Dream Life – Believe, Achieve and Receive and Extraordinary Life of Passion and Purpose…

Your Dream Life Just Ahead!

Visit her websites:

www.DiscoverandLiveYourDreamLife.com

www.FriendlyTipsforFlyingTrips.com

www.TheeMarQueeEnterprises.com

www.WitnessPerformingArts.com

www.Christinexercise.com

www.MarQueMunday.com

www.PilateswithMarQue.com

www.Called4Purpose.com

www.MarQueLV.com

Book inquiries please contact me at info@discoverandliveyourdreamlife.com

Looking forward to connecting with you.

Made in the USA
Monee, IL
04 November 2022

17118726R00075